KU-176-357

TENERIFE

Text, photographs, design, lay-out and printing, entirely created by the technical department of EDITORIAL ESCUDO DE ORO, S.A.

Rights of total or partial reproduction and translation reserved.

Copyright of this edition for photographs and text:
© EDITORIAL ESCUDO DE ORO, S.A.
Palaudarias, 26 - 08004 Barcelona (Spain).

5th Edition

I.S.B.N. 84-378-1386-7

The printing of this book was completed
in the workshops of
FISA - ESCUDO DE ORO, S.A.
PALAUDARIAS, 26 - 08004 Barcelona (Spain)

Dep. Legal B. 31159-1997

A tile depicting the struggle of the aboriginal inhabitants of Tenerife against the conquerors.

TENERIFE: BRIEF HISTORICAL ACCOUNT, CLIMATE AND GEOGRAPHICAL LOCATION

The island of Tenerife, like the rest of the Canaries, is a volcanic outcrop on a Precambrian crystalline insular shelf that appeared in the Atlantic opposite the Sahara millions of years ago. It is the largest island in the archipelago, with a surface area of 2,053 km². Its terrain is also the most rugged, with Anaga, Teno and La Rasca marking the three points of its triangular shape. The mountain range that runs the breadth of the island and culminates in the Teide divides Tenerife into two clearly differentiated parts: the north — fertile, humid and covered with woods; and the south — desertlike with ochre and earth colours predominating. This is why Tenerife has been called the "island of the two faces".

Tenerife's latitude and proximity to the Sahara would have spelled a desert climate were it not for the influence of the sea and the winds. In winter, the Gulf Stream warms the atmosphere, whereas in summer, the trade winds cool it. The temperatures vary only slightly throughout the year, the minimum in February being 17° C and the maximum in August being 24.8° C, so that Tenerife's climate may be described as warm-hot.

The origins of the island's present-day population can be traced back to events that took place during the reign of the Catholic Monarchs who had ordered Alonso Fernández de Lugo to conquer La Palma and Tenerife. Lugo succeeded in bringing La Palma under his control in 1493 after a series of pacts with the island's native kings. However, his diplomatic tactics did not bear the same results in Tenerife and when war was declared he suffered his first defeat at the hands of the Guanches in the Acentejo ravine. He later succeeded in subjugating the *mencey* (tribal chieftain or king) of Taoro and, on the 25th December 1495, conquered the remaining tribes in Taoro, Tacoronte and Daute. The conquest of the island was completed. And so it was that from the 16th century onwards, the indigenous Guanche population began to intermarry with the successive waves of immigrants arriving from the Iberian peninsula.

The Guanches or ancient settlers of the island of Tenerife, were a people whose origins are lost in legend. It is said that they came from Atlantis, the island swallowed up by the sea, and that they were tall and blond.

From the Plaza de España a train leaves on a tour of the city.

Plaza de España, Santa Cruz de Tenerife.

Plaza de la Candelaria, Santa Cruz de Tenerife.

Punta de Anaga, where we find one of the lighthouses on the island which can be reached only on foot.

Detail of the port of Santa Cruz de Tenerife.

In the 15th century, the Spanish conquerors discovered a native population who was still living in the Stone Age: they had not heard of metals, they mummified their dead and on feast days painted themselves with clay stamps. Surprisingly, identical stamps were discovered in Mexico.

Their language, of unknown origin, bears some relation to dialects used by the Berbers and Haitians.

According to J. Alvarez Delgado the word "guanche" derives from *Achineh*, which was the name given to the island by the natives. In this case "guanche" would mean "inhabitant of Achineh". The large number of skulls found bear a striking resemblance to the Cro-Magnon type of man with, however, certain Semitic and Berber characteristics.

The Guanches lived in caves and buried their dead in them. They dressed in skins and ate meat, cheese and "gofio" (toasted wheat or oat meal). Their utensils (millstones, cheese moulds and pottery) were very rudimentary with scarcely any decoration.

They worshipped the sun, moon, stars and other natural elements; they believed in spirits (the evil spirit was called *Guayota)*, the supreme God, however, was *Achamán*, the Almighty.

Close-up in Parque Marítimo César Manrique, opened in 1995, in Santa Cruz de Tenerife.

Plaza de España, Santa Cruz de Tenerife, where we find the Chapter House of Tenerife building and beside it the Post and Telegraph Office.

SANTA CRUZ DE TENERIFE AND LA LAGUNA: THE NORTHERN ROUTE

Founded in 1493 by the captain-general and governor Alonso Fernández de Lugo, the city of Santa Cruz, from where the conquest of the island was begun in 1495, was formerly a small town and serving port La Laguna, the capital of the island at that time. Because of its geographical situation and the important role its harbour acquired in the itineraries of the Spanish fleets that sailed to America, it soon became the coveted prey of pirates and English corsairs. This led to various defence fortifications being built along its coastline, such as St. Christopher's castle (1570), St. John's castle (1648) and Paso Alto castle from which the pirate Blake (1657) and Admiral Nelson (1797) were successfully fended off and defeated. Santa Cruz port was already considered to be the most important on the island at the time. In 1721, the military headquarters was set up in the city which now had complete control over maritime traffic and especially the trade carried on with the Americas.

This beautiful and hospitable city of the Canaries, situated on the north-eastern coast of Tenerife, sits at the foot of a mountain range that gently slopes down to the sea. From its beginnings as a port, it slowly grew up the mountain side, that is to say, in a south-north direction. It was in the 18th century and particularly in the 19th century that the city began its expansion from the city centre situated in the old quarter of Cabo, in the port itself, towards the north-east, acquiring a radial pattern. However, from 1950 onwards, the city experienced a spectacular growth attributed for the most part to the building of the La Laguna road which has become the city's main arterial route. At the point where it enters the city, it becomes the so-called Rambla de Pulido.

The city's main buildings and administrative centre are located in the José Antonio and Anaga seaside avenues, the areas around Candelaria square and Plaza de España and the port. Two main roads run through the city centre, the Rambla and the Tres de Mayo avenue, going east and west respectively, which connect the port to the coastal roads and the motorway leading to Los Rodeos airport. New

Panorama of Santa Cruz de Tenerife.

residential areas have been built on the slopes of the Anaga mountain range, making the city look like a large amphitheatre.

Santa Cruz de Tenerife boasts many places that are well worth a visit. For those who wish to begin with the city's most noteworthy monuments, we suggest they start with the church of the Immaculate Conception (1502), which is considered to be the oldest religious building in the city. After being destroyed in a fire it was reconstructed to the original design in the 17th century. It has a low nave and four aisles, its slender belfry, built on a square groundplan, looming high above the church. Inside, the altar of Our Lady of Carmen, of polychrome wood, as well as two beautiful sculptures can be admired: Our Lady of Sorrows, by Luján Pérez and the Immaculate Conception, considered to be the oldest on the island. In the chapel of St. James is the Cross of the Conquest and the flags that were captured during Admiral Nelson's failed attack in 1797.

The church of St. Francis, restored in the 18th century, which has a colonial main front is also of great interest. The Municipal Fine Arts Museum has been housed in the adjoining buildings where

Detail of the García Sanabria Park in Santa Cruz de Tenerife.

The Santa Cruz de Tenerife city carnival is one of the most popular tourist attractions.

the exhibits comprise the works of Canarian artists in particular as well as the works of renowned painters such as Brueghel, Ribera, Madrazo, Van Loo, etc.

The best of the city's civil architecture is to be seen in the Casino (social club) of Tenerife which has mural paintings by many of the island's artists and the Carta palace (18th century), both of which are in Candelaria square. The Neoclassical buildings of the Military Headquarters and the Guimerá theatre date from the first half of the 19th century.

Different aspects of the famous Santa Cruz de Tenerife carnival.

Today, Santa Cruz is a modern city full of buildings in innovative architectural style that have been designed and built by architects of great repute.

The city boasts a large number of squares, such as Weyler square, where the Military Headquarters is situated, and in the centre of which there is a beautiful fountain built by Italian artists; Paz square, with its beautiful gardens and Candelaria square, in the heart of the city, which is presided over by the monument known as ''The triumph of the Candelaria,'' representing the appearance of Our Lady to the Guanches on Chimisay beach. This marvellous

View of part of the port of Santa Cruz de Tenerife and behind it the Anaga Coast.

work was sculpted in marble by the great Italian artist, Antonio Canova, in 1778.

From here, going past España square, we can make our way to the port, one of Spain's most important. It is situated in a wide bay surrounded by the Anaga mountain range, where the city nestles, and is an important centre of maritime traffic and communications between Europe, Africa and America. Vessels from all parts of the world dock in it and cruisers carrying tourists regularly drop anchor here throughout the year.

Finally, our introduction to Tenerife and brief history of the Canary Islands would not be complete without a visit to the Archaeological Museum where there is an excellent collection of remains of Guanche culture on display. A typical Guanche burial has been recreated with some of the mummies found in the excavations.

A walk through the huge García Sanabria park, located between Méndez Núñez street and Rambla del General Franco, will give us an idea of its trapezoid in shape area, stocked with a great variety of exotic plants and trees.

The visitor to the capital of the island will immediately be aware of a lively, festive atmosphere in the streets which are lined with shops, hotels and all

Playa de Taganana, Santa Cruz de Tenerife.

manner of commercial enterprises. This constant activity is heightened in the month of Febuary when the famous carnival of Tenerife is celebrated and during which time the city is a riot of light and colour. The entire population participates in the festivities wearing the most fantastic disguises and for six days walks the streets to the frenzied rhythm of tropical music. This important festival attracts a large number of visitors who take part in what can be considered as one of the Canary Islands' most important events.

The feast of the Holy Cross, which commemorates the founding of the city, is celebrated at the beginning of May. Although the festivities last the whole month, the 3rd May is the most important day when the city banner is taken out in parade and a competition of floral croses is held.

The north-bound motorway out of Santa Cruz will enable us to reach *La Laguna,* only 9 km away, in just a few minutes. It is the oldest city on the island, being the very first that the governor Fernández de Lugo founded. It served as the capital city until the 18th century and this is apparent in the

El Prix, a small fishing harbour.

A picturesque detail of El Prix.

beautiful buildings and stately layout. A large number of monuments deserve to be visited. We can begin our tour with the cathedral, which was once the Remedios parish church. Its construction was begun in 1515, with numerous reforms carried out during the 17th and 18th centuries. Its final structure, however, emerged only in the early 20th century. Of great interest is the sober Neoclassical main front. It houses many works of art: pieces of silver craftsmanship from the 18th century and carvings by the Tenerife born sculptor Fernando Estévez (1788-1854); of great artistic value is a beautiful statue of Our Lady of Candelaria. Behind the high altar is the tomb of the conqueror, Alonso Fernández de Lugo.

Also highly recommended is the parish church of the Immaculate Conception (16th century) where the visitor can admire the polychrome wood coffered ceiling of the 16th and 17th centuries; the church of the Royal Hospital of Our Lady with its extraordinary high altar; the church of St. Augustine which has a cloister considered to be one of the city's best architectural works; the church of St. Dominic decorated with frescoes and the monastery of St. Francis where the famous Christ of La Laguna is venerated.

As regards civil architecture, the Bishop's palace and the Nava Grimón palace, built by the Marquises of Villanueva, deserve special mention. The latter, together with the Town hall and the convent of St. Catherine, form a magnificent block that stands opposite the famous Adelantado square. La Laguna's importance, however, derives not only from the fact that it is the foremost historical and artistic centre but also the university city, par excellence, of the archipelago. Its modern buildings and colleges stand on a huge esplanade. The university fully deserves the considerable prestige it enjoys.

Only 3 km from La Laguna is Los Rodeos airport, used mainly for flights within the Canaries.

Starting at both Santa Cruz and La Laguna are good roads that will take us into the north-western part of the island. San Andrés, only 8 km from the capital, can be reached by taking the road leading out of the capital and go-

The Playa de las Teresitas, next to San Andrés.

General view of Puerto de la Cruz.

ing past the yacht club, Paso Alto and the huge harbour. It is a small fishing village with streets full of bars and restaurants that also conserves a part of the ruins of a circular fortress destroyed thirty years ago by flooding. The famous 1.5 km long *Las Teresitas beach,* for which tonnes of fine sand were brought across from the Sahara, can be seen from here.

From here we have a choice of two routes; one in the direction of the coast going past *Punta de los Organos,* which affords a magnificent panoramic view,

arriving shortly afterwards at *Igueste de San Andrés,* a small village near which megalithic settlements and other remains were discovered.

The second route takes us along a winding road to the picturesque *Taganana* village, famous for the fine needlework produced by its women. In the nearby hamlet of *Almáciga* is a hermitage dedicated to Our Lady of Begoña which dates from the 17th century. The road to Taganana starts in *El Bailadero,* a pass in the heart of the mountain range, and from which *Monte*

The Martiánez beach, with the famous lake and swimming pools in the background.

de las Mercedes, a mere 9 km away can be reached. This area is of particular interest because it boasts one of the most important reserves of laurisilva, an almost extinct species from the Tertiary age.

From La Laguna, we can visit the *Cruz del Carmen hermitage* and *Taborno*, with its unforgettably beautiful view, as well as *Bajamar*, in the direction of the coast, which is an important tourist centre having natural pools along the seashore, and *Punta del Hidalgo*, both of which are almost linked together by *Arenal Beach*.

ON THE WAY TO EL PUERTO DE LA CRUZ

We could begin our journey to El Puerto de la Cruz from La Laguna. After passing through one of the flattest and greenest regions of Tenerife, we arrive at *Tacoronte*, well-known for its wines and whose vineyards contrast sharply with the large areas of thick woods, such as *Agua García*. The characteristic appearance of its relief outline and its abundance of caves made it one of the most densely inhabited by Guanches before the conquest, as is borne out by

Panorama of Puerto de la Cruz.

Lake Martiánez at sunset.

A detail of the beautiful Martiánez swimming pools.

Lake Martiánez. Different views. ▷

the human remains and funeral urns found here.

Today, Tacoronte has become an important tourist centre thanks to its ideal situation near the coast. It has some estate developments, such as in *Mesa del Mar.* Not far from here is *El Prix,* a tiny and picturesque fishing village well worth a visit. A little way from the town stands the parish church of St. Catherine of Tacoronte, built in 1664. It houses some reredoses and statues of which the statue of Our Lady of Carmen, sculpted by Luján Pérez, deserves special mention. In the so-called shrine of Christ, which was once the chapel of an Augustinian monastery, is the Christ of Sorrows, a 17th-century polychrome carving that is venerated all over the island and which has led to Tacoronte's importance as a religious centre.

Continuing our itinerary on the motorway, we arrive at *El Sauzal,* a small town clearly divided into two parts: the higher, covered with the vineyards that annually produce high quality wines, and the lower or coastal strip that has become an amusement place for tourists with its estate developments — such as Los Angeles —, hotels, villas and all manner of residences, which ex-

The recreational complex of Lake Martiánez, designed by César Manrique.

ude life all the year round, including the winter months.

Following the route to El Puerto de la Cruz, we now approach the historical small towns of *La Matanza de Acentejo* and *La Victoria de Acentejo*. It was here that the bloodiest battles were fought between the Guanches and the Spanish.

In the spring of 1494, on precisely the 31st May, Alonso Fernández de Lugo, convinced that *mencey* Bencomo would not quietly surrender to his forces, decided to attack the Guanches. He led his men towards Taoro which was Bencomo's territory. Bencomo, who knew of the Spanish General's plans, ordered his allies not to put up any resistance to the General's troops, allowing them to pass through their territories and so walk into the ambush he was preparing. The Spanish army, not encountering any resistance, soon reached La Orotova, from where, in need of victuals, they took with them a large number of the cattle that were left grazing in the rich pastures, before they continued on their way to Acentejo. The Guanches, however, who had followed them closely, spying on all their movements, lay in wait for Fernández de Lugo and his soldiers in the *Acentejo ravine*.

It was Tinguaro, the brother of Ben-

Detail of the Plaza de Europa, Puerto de la Cruz, from where we can enjoy beautiful views.

como, who let the Spanish troops enter the ravine and waited patiently until they had reached its most difficult and inhospitable part. It was then that the Guanches whistled to the cattle that began to stampede. In the ensuing confusion the Spanish were unable to reorganise themselves to face the unexpected attack of the natives. And so began the bloody battle in which Fernández de Lugo's army suffered total defeat. According to the chronicles, more than 900 men died in the battle although it is believed that the real number of victims was around 2,000. Even Fernández de Lugo was injured in the mouth and lost his horse.

It appears that he saved his life only because he changed his red cape for the blue one of a soldier who the Guanches persued and killed, mistaking him for the conqueror. Lugo returned to the Azaña camp and later to the island of Grand Canary having suffered the biggest defeat ever in the history of the conquest of the Canary Islands.
The hard battle and its bloody sequel led to this place being called ''La Matanza de Acentejo'' (The Acentejo Slaughter), where two totally different worlds clashed. This, however, has long been forgotten and the place has recovered its old splendour, presided over by its immense vineyards and

banana plantations. La Matanza is a tranquil farming community which produces traditional red wines.

When Fernández de Lugo recovered from the wounds and from the terrible defeat inflicted on him and his troops in Acentejo, he took up the fight against the natives once again. It was on the 24th December of that same year that he and his men marched towards the Acentejo ravine, taking advantage of the arrival of a Spanish ship bringing provisions under the command of Lope Hernández de la Guerra. With the latter's help, Lugo attacked Bencomo and Acaymo, *mencey* of Tacoronte, who between them commanded some 5,000 Guanches, divided into two bands. This battle was as cruel and bloody as the former one, although this time the Spanish did better, losing only 64 soldiers as compared with the 2,000 Guanches who lost their lives. Bencomo decided to withdraw with his men to the Hondo ravine and this provoked a shout of Victory!, Victory! from the Spanish soldiers celebrating their opponents' defeat. This cry later became the name of the town that was founded here.

Puerto de la Cruz at nightfall.

Parish church of San Amaro (16th century), La Paz, Puerto de la Cruz.

After this memorable triumph in July 1496, Bencomo surrendered to Fernández de Lugo to avoid further bloodshed. He was made a subject of the Catholic Monarchs to whom he paid hommage and vowed obedience. The *mencey* of Taoro, like most of the Guanche princes was sent to Spain where he was taken from one city to another.

And so ended the conquest of the Canary Islands and ninety-two years of hard battles and clashes between the island's natives and the Spanish conquerors.

At the site of the last battle, Fernández de Lugo ordered that a hermitage dedicated to Our Lady of Victory be built as a sign of gratitude for the final victory. According to the inhabitants of this town, the majestic pine tree that stands beside the small chapel was initially used as the bell-tower, as the church's first bell was hung from it.

We recommend that you stop awhile in the outskirts of this town, where a very primitive type of pottery is still made using Guanche techniques.

The road now goes past the village of *St. Ursula*, whose church has a beautiful carving of St. Rita by the Canary Island sculptor, Estévez. The scenery starts to get lusher, reminding us that we are nearing the Orotava

Detail of the promenade, Puerto de la Cruz.

The beaches of Puerto de la Cruz provide a haven of peace for the traveller. Detail of Playa Jardín.

valley. A road turns off towards the *Humboldt vista point,* from where this famous German explorer comtemplated the imcomparable beauty of the Orotava and the Teide peak.

EL PUERTO DE LA CRUZ

El Puerto de la Cruz, with a surface area of 9.7 km², lies on the northern coast of the island of Tenerife. It is one of the main tourist resorts in the archipelago and one of the most important in Spain, vying in prestige with the resorts of Benidorm, Torremolinos, Ibiza and Majorca.

In 1648, King Philip IV united this town, which at that time was very small, with La Orotava city for which it would serve as the port. El Puerto de la Cruz soon became one of the most important ports on the island from which much of the wine produced in Tenerife was exported. This activity was heightened at the start of this century with the construction of a new dock for exporting the surplus bananas grown on the island.

In spite of being a modern tourist resort with all manner of amenities, El Puerto de la Cruz still conserves some of the buildings belonging to its historical past. Of its most important monuments, those deserving special mention are: the parish church of Our Lady of the Peña de Francia, in Quintana street, built in the early 17th century with some features of the Baroque style. Its beautiful high altar, the work of the artist Luis de la Cruz, various statues of saints also dating from this period and objects of gold and silver craftsmanship from the 17th and 18th centuries are worthy of admiration. A visit to the hermitage dedicated to St. Telmo is also a must. It was constructed in 1628 and restored many times due mainly to the fire in which it was almost completely destroyed in 1788. It still houses the statue of St. Pedro González Telmo, patron-saint of fishermen.

The city still preserves some of its stately houses in beautiful typically Canary Island architectural style, with carved wooden balconies and courtyards overflowing with plants.

At the extreme southern end of the Luis Lavaggi promenade stands the small castle of St. Philip dating from the 17th century. It was a defence fortress and serves as a reminder of its belligerent past replete with stories of pirates and corsairs.

Very little remains of the once obscure Puerto de la Cruz with its well tended

The Castle of San Felipe.

Calle Quintana, Puerto de la Cruz.

streets overrun by the heavy commercial traffic of its port. Today it is a big town with smart buildings whose livelihood proceeds almost exclusively from the tourists who come to bask on its beaches, enjoy the climate and contemplate the landscapes.

There are a large number of hotels, estate developments and other types of accommodation available to visitors. In addition, El Puerto de la Cruz boasts a wide variety of restaurants, cafeterias, night clubs and various amenities and facilities to provide the tourist with hours of fun and relaxation.

The most attractive spot on its coast where almost all holiday-makers flock is undoubtedly *Martiánez beach,* situated in the very centre of El Puerto de la Cruz. It was here that the architect César Manrique built an extraordinary recreational area along the sea front, next to the caves once inhabited by the Guanches, which covers an area of 33,000 m². It comprises a huge artificial lake, 15,000 m² –in which there have been installed a restaurant, bars, solariums, etc. and several swimming pools along the Paseo de Colón, stretching as far as the Plaza de los Reyes Católicos. Here too is the famous Andrómeda dance hall built under the water, considered to be one of the most luxurious and exotic in the whole of Europe.

View of part of the gardens of the beautiful Taoro Park, where we can find the Puerto de la Cruz casino and a pleasant terrace bar.

El Puerto de la Cruz still conserves its small fishing port located behind Las Lonjas street, right beside the market and very close to the Town Hall. Of great interest is the fishermen's quarter that still retains its original character thanks to its tiny, secluded squares and its narrow streets.

The Taoro road leads to a park of the same name and a small bullring of interest to the tourist.

Finally, we must not leave El Puerto de la Cruz without first having visited the famous Botanical Gardens and "Loro Parque" (Parrot Park), two delightful places where we can spend some very pleasant hours.

The *Botanical Gardens* or *Jardín de Aclimatación* (acclimatization), as it is also known, stands in Durazno. It was once the royal gardens.

The Botanical Gardens date back to the 18th century, to 1788 or 1790, when the Marquis of Villanueva del Prado, Don Alonso de Nava y Benítez de Lugo, at the time an important personality in Tenerife, wished to have a huge park boasting the greatest number of plants, typical of the Canary Islands flora as well as those representative of the various species to be found in the world. Naturalists and garden designers were invited to the island to take charge of designing and building what is today one of Spain's most important natural museums. It contains from the most exotic and striking to the humblest examples of the plant kingdom; from the tiniest plants to the largest trees: heather, araucaria, beech, Canary pine, rosemary, "tajinaste", bushes, euphorbia, prickly pear, chestnut, and many others. There is a splendid rubber tree that occupies a privileged position presiding over the gardens. The variety of species growing in this garden come from regions that are climatically and geographically different. However, the balanced climate that Tenerife enjoys compensates for the various climatic features of the countries of origin.

On the other side of the city is the beautiful beach, Playa Jardín, equipped with modern facilities, which provides visitors with an opportunity to eat in a pleasant terrace restaurant in the beach gardens. Two hundred metres away we find the "Loro Parque" (Parrot Park), beautiful gardens and amenities set amidst luxuriant subtropical vegetation. In perfect harmony with nature, the park is home to the largest collection of parrots in the world: about 230 species, or a total of 1,300 birds. It is a large reserve for endangered species, as many of them have been disappearing due to the destruction of their natural habitats. The park also puts on various attractions such as the "Parrot Show" where you can appreciate the countless skills of these birds who can ride bicycles, play basketball, roller skate and walk on

General view of Playa Jardín, in the Punta Brava area, Puerto de la Cruz.

"Loro Park".

tightropes. Another spectacle is the "Black Continent", a free flying performance by the parrots followed by a function in the "Parrot Vision" area: "the crazy world of man seen through the eyes of the parrot."

This fabulous park also has other attractions like the *Dolphin aquarium,* one of the best in the world, and which boasts shows of an international standard; the sea lion show, the *"Orchidarium"* where you can see 2,000 orchids in bloom; the crocodile viewpoint; an aquarium where you can watch the sharks and other fish swimming to and fro; as well as other water shows. "Loro Parque" is carrying out the important task of protecting and looking after nature, and its maintenance and care of the animals is unsurpassed.

And do not forget that the Parrot Park provides its visitors with a free, easy-to-spot train which starts from the Avenida Colón and makes a tour of the Puerto de la Cruz on the way to the facilities. The trains leave every 15 minutes and operate during the opening hours of the Parrot Park.

*Traditional balconies of La Orotava
decorated for the Corpus Christi festival.*

LA OROTAVA

From El Puerto de la Cruz, a road leads into the interior and the Orotava valley, one of the most beautiful spots on the island. Thick vegetation, like a mantle of different shades of green, covers the northern slopes of the Teide over an area of 62 km^2. In the centre is the picturesque town of La Orotava, founded at the beginning of the Spanish conquest of the island. Between the 17th and 18th centuries, La Orotava enjoyed the favour of the nobility, as can be appreciated from the numerous stately houses with rich inner courtyards still conserved in their original splendour, and the old palaces adorned with their elaborately carved, large, wooden balconies. Of artistic interest is the parish church of the Immaculate Conception, of which the original building dating from the 16th century was destroyed by earth tremors registered in 1705 when the volcano in the southern region of Güimar erupted. It stands as an example of an extraordinary Baroque style, constructed between 1768 and 1788, with an outstanding main front flanked by two towers. The church has a nave and two aisles with barrel vaulting, except in the transept which has a cupola. The Neoclassical tabernacle of the high

La Orotava: «House of the Balconies», with its filigree work.

altar, of jasper and marble, was sculpted in Genoa by Giovanni Gaggini in 1823, from a sketch drawn by Ventura Rodríguez. Worthy of admiration are some statues of a remarkable quality: Our Lady of Sorrows, St. John and St. Magdalene by the Canarian sculptor, José Luján Pérez (18th century); and St. Peter by Rodríguez de la Oliva. There is also a Gothic monstrance of gilded silver.

Another important monument is the church of St. John, where there are two noteworthy works by Luján as well as an impressive Christ tied to the column by Roldán.

In the centre of the town is the famous square, the ''Orotava Balcony'' or Town Hall square, embellished with palm trees and flower beds. A very deep-rooted custom of the town is to cover the streets with carpets of flowers during the Corpus Christi celebrations. The most spectacular and famous decoration to be seen is in the Town Hall square where, however, the flower petals are replaced by ground earth or volcanic sand of different colours brought from Las Cañadas, with which an enormous carpet of eucharistic symbols is composed.

A carpet of different coloured earth which
is laid for the Corpus Christi festival.

View of La Orotava; Puerto de la Cruz in
the background.

Savannah grass, one of the typical plant species of the Teide.

THE TEIDE

Originating at La Orotava is a twisting road that will take us through a wooded area to *Aguamansa,* and then climb to *El Portillo* (2,020 m) which, together with *Boca Tauce* to the south west, are the natural mountain passes providing access to *Las Cañadas.* Only 14 km from El Portillo is the ''Roques'' vista point which overlooks the Ucanca valley and is very near the state-owned hotel (''Parador''). The ''Dorsal road'', built in the early 1940's to connect Santa Cruz and La Laguna with the Teide, also ends at Las Cañadas. This alternative route runs through one of

the most attractive spots on the island: *Monte de la Esperanza,* where the typical pitch pine tree grows; its picturesque ''tea'' or Canary pinewood is traditionally used for the beautiful and famous Tenerife balconies. Some vista points, such as Cumbres, Diablillo (1,600 m), Ortuño (1,802 m) and Ayosa (2,000 m), offer extraordinary panoramic views. Further on is the Meteorological Observatory of Izaña (2,386 m) and the Astronomical Observatory of the Teide.
The visit to Las Cañadas del Teide, an enormous crater or volcanic cavity in the shape of a cauldron, will surely arouse the tourist's surprise and amaze-

An idyllic valley at the foot of the Teide.

*The so-called lunar landscape of the
Ucanca plain on the slopes of the Teide.*

Mountain, which merge together in the landscape; or the famous Yellow Stones, or the area known as "Azulejos", where greenish tones predominate, due the iron oxide in the soil. Other sites that we highly recommend visiting are: White Mountain, formed by the accumulation of "lapilli" or glassy volcanic stones and the "Pilas" or small lagoons which trap the waters from the melting snows in the spring.

A difference of opinion still persists regarding the formation of this great crater. Some believe that it was brought about by a continuous sinking registered in this area in ancient times, whilst others feel it was caused by erosion. There is no doubt, however, that Las Cañadas del Teide are 300,000 years old. The most probable hypothesis advanced is that there were two immense craters divided by the so-called Roques García, which were gradually filled during the continuous eruptions.

The incomparable beauty of Las Cañadas and the need to preserve it in its original state led to its being declared a National Park, covering a total area of 13,571 Ha, on 22nd February 1954.

Los Roques viewpoint.

The eroded and cosmic appearance of the
Ucanca valley.

In the Teide National Park we can enjoy an unforgettable stay at the Parador Nacional.

We arrive at the foot of the Teide by following the only road there is leading to this spectacular volcanic spot; its majesty has undoubtedly contributed to Tenerife's distinctive character from ancient times. The highest point on this enormous volcano which looms over the island is the Teide peak, 3,718 m above sea level. It is thus the highest peak in Spain, rising well above Aneto peak (3,404 m) in the Pyrenees and Mulhacén peak (3,478 m) in the Sierra Nevada.

The experts seem to agree that, unlike Las Cañadas, the Teide was formed by the superposition of different volcanos

(Mount Chahorra or Old Peak, 3,106 m high, etc.) that were active until the end of the 18th century.

Although the Chinyero volcano erupted in 1909, throwing up smoke and lava, the eruption of Mount Chahorra in 1798 is considered to be the most recent important one. It began on the 9th June and lasted three months. At this time, a series of secondary conduits, known as ''the nostrils of the Teide'' were formed on the sides of mount Chahorra. This could mean that the main conduit or expansion conduit was blocked off with layer upon layer of solidified lava.

Landscape of Los Roques, in Las Cañadas.

The mouth of the crater, with a diameter of 80 m, still sends gases shooting up at a temperature of almost 90° C, commonly referred to as "solfataras".

There are two ways of going up the Teide, on foot, following the normal route taken by ramblers, which starts on Mount Blanca, or by cable car, which operates from morning to evening, leaving from the base of the volcano, at a height of 2,356 m, and climbing up to "la Rambleta" (3,555 m), from where, the summit is within a walking distance of approximately 25 minutes. A marvellous panoramic view of the whole island can be enjoyed from here, which on clear days includes almost all the islands of the archipelago.

There is little doubt that the most outstanding feature of all these spots is their wealth of geological formations; however, we must not forget that they are also the habitat of numerous forms of life. Lovers of Botany will find a true "floral paradise" with unique species belonging to the Canary Islands as well as those species that only grow in the park area. The most noteworthy species are: the famous "Guanche rose bush", pinkish in colour, and the "Teide violet" which grows most pro-

The cable car which goes up to «La Rambleta» from the base of the volcano.

Pine woods dot the landscape of the Teide.

ately to call it the "sugar lump".
The Teide has always left a profound and lasting impression on all those who have visited the island. From ancient times, the mariners that sailed the sea around the islands were surprised by the enormous size of this volcano whose silhouette can be discerned many miles away from Tenerife. The Greek historian, Herodotus, on his voyages along the coast of Northern Africa named it "Atlas", whilst others called it the "column of heaven". It would be difficult to imagine the tremendous earth movements that preceded the creation of such unusual forms. However, it is thanks to those cataclysmic events that we can today behold one of the world's most marvellous sights.

After our visit to Las Cañadas del Teide National Park we can return to La Orotava to continue our tour of the island.

The majestic Teide will however remain with us, and not only in our thoughts but accompanying us all over the island, above which it towers majestically and is clearly visible from all angles.

View from the Ortuño viewpoint.

The Teide, named «Atlanta» by Herodotus.

The Los Realejos coastal area—the "Playa de Socorro".

LOS REALEJOS AND ICOD DE LOS VINOS

A few kilometers from El Puerto de la Cruz is Los Realejos made up of a lower and an upper small town, *Realejo Bajo* and *Realejo Alto*. Realejo Alto is a place of great historical importance because it was here that the Guanches surrendered to Alonso Fernández de Lugo in 1496. A church, St. James' of Realejo Alto, was built to commemorate this event and it is the oldest on the island, dating from the end of the 15th century. Inside, some Flemish reredoses can be admired; worthy of mention on the outside is the slender bell-tower. According to tradition, at least one of the bells was donated by the Catholic Monarchs.

In the church square of the parish of Our Lady of Carmen stands a monument dedicated to the renowned Canarian writer and historian Viera y Clavijo (1731-1812).

There is an interesting dragon tree to be seen in Realejo Bajo. The church of Our Lady of the Immaculate Conception is also highly recommended, where an exquistely polychrome, 17th-

Typical details.

The ancient dragon tree, with picturesque Canarian buildings.

century, carved wooden Baroque reredos as well as a jasper baptismal font have been preserved.

Continuing westwards on our journey through beautiful coastal landscapes, we will first arrive at the small town of *San Juan de la Rambla,* and then at *Icod de los Vinos.* The latter is famous for its select wines. It was founded in 1501 and still retains the old quarter with a number of buildings in the purest Canarian style; its square and gardens, such as the Lorenzo Cáceres park with its majestic and characteristic bay trees deserve special mention. Of great artistic interest are the buildings of the

Town Hall and the parish church of St. Mark, whose construction dates from the 15th and 16th centuries, with the exception of the tower that was built in the 17th century. The Renaissance doorway is noteworthy. Inside the church there is a splendid Baroque reredos from the 17th century, objects of gold and silver and important sculptures, such as the statue of St. Diego of Alcalá, the work of the Granadine sculptor, Pedro de Mena (1628-1688).

Other monuments of interest are: the monastery of the Franciscans where the highly venerated statue of the

Two enchanting details of Icod de los Vinos.

The ancient dragon tree of Icod de los Vinos.

Christ of the Waters is to be found; the monastery of St. Augustine and the chapel of Our Lady of Sorrows.

It must not be forgotten that the ancient dragon tree, the oldest and most famous of those that remain in the Canary Islands, can be seen here. This tree grows very slowly, its trunk gradually dividing from a single bole into smaller branches. Its leaves are shaped like lance heads and bunch together in tufts at the tips of the branches. Dragon trees live for centuries. There is no exact record of the age of the Icod dragon tree; the local inhabitants, however, say that it is between 2,500 and 3,000 years old.

The dragon tree is a sacred tree from which the Guanches extracted sap ("dragon tree blood") which they used, among other things, as a healing potion. In ancient times, Roman women used it as a cosmetic, whilst in the Middle Ages, it was used for making ointments and in the treatment of leprosy.

Nearby is *Monte Castro wood* and *San Marcos beach*, from which one of the best views of the Teide can be enjoyed.

View of «Las Cruces» and a detail of the coast.

General view of Garachico.

GARACHICO: ON THE WAY TO THE WESTERNMOST POINT OF THE ISLAND

At a distance of approximately 4 km from Icod de los Vinos is the picturesque town of Garachico, founded at the beginning of the Spanish conquest of the island. Its port soon became the centre for wine exports to other countries, rivalling that of El Puerto de la Cruz in importance, long before they were both displaced by Santa Cruz de Tenerife.

However, the history of this small town was marked by a catastrophy in the spring of 1706, when an eruption blew open the enormous craters in Mount Bermeja and Mount Atalaya, throwimg up great streams of lava that destroyed it completely and permanently closed its port, forming a large peninsula.

The new city was built on this stretch of land. Some buildings dating from this period, in the construction of which black lava stone was used, are still to be seen. Of the most remarkable monuments, those deserving special mention are: the San Miguel castle built in 1575, with its marvellous entrance archway richly decorated with coats of arms which belonged at one time to the Count of Gomera; the church of Saint Anne (18th century) erected on the foundations of an earlier construction, where a Rococo reredos dedicated to

The Castle of San Miguel in Garachico.

St. Joachim, a work by Luján Pérez, can be admired; and finally some old palaces, such as the Baroque palace of the Marquis of Adeje (17th century). The landscape on this side of the coast was completely modified. Proof of this are the strata or folds of lava more than a hundred metres long and between four and eight metres wide, where a number of natural pools have formed. Rising out of the sea, a short distance from the coast, is the Garachico rock which has become a symbol of the town.

Only 6 km away from Garachico is the small town, *Los Silos,* surrounded by huge banana plantations, and where coffee and tropical plants are also grown thanks to the excellent climate of the region. A visit to the parish church of Our Lady of Light is highly recommended. It contains a beautiful Baroque carving of the Most Holy Christ of Mercy, attributed to the sculptor Juan de Mesa, one of the most outstanding representatives of the 17th-century Sevillian school.

This area abounds in places of exceptional scenic beauty, such as *Cuevas Negras, Roque Blanco, Bosques de Aguas* and *Valle de la tierra del trigo.* Along the coast are beaches and coves

View of part of the Puerta de Tierra
gardens in Garachico.

Church of St Anne, Garachico.

Punta de Teno and behind it the Giants' Cliff.

that are easily reached, such as La Caleta cove and El Puertito beach.

Continuing on the same road which ends at Punta de Teno, the westernmost point of the island, we arrive at the small town of *Buenavista* founded in the 16th century. It is here and in the surrounding areas that we shall contemplate one of the wildest and most abrupt landscapes on the island, where steep and spectacular cliffs hang above the sea. The town has a beautiful church with valuable reredoses and Mudejar coffered ceilings, a carving of St. Francis by Alonso Cano (1601-1667), as well as some stately houses of the 17th and 18th centuries.

On our return to Garachico we can visit the famous "Puerta de Tierra" gardens which, with their great variety of flowers, are a miniature paradise.

THE FLORA

The exuberant flora in this region justifies more detailed mention of some of the most important species to be found on the island.

Tenerife was a port of call for voyages to the Orient, South and East Africa and America. This factor, together with its unchanging subtropical climate led to many different plant species being im-

Specimens of the flora of Tenerife, among them the olivia miniata.

Gazania.

ported, which are now to be found in the many gardens all over the island, such as the La Orotova Botanical Gardens and the L. Cáceres garden in Icod de los Vinos. A great variety of plants are also to be seen adorning the squares and parks in the cities — such as García Sanabria Park and La Granja Park, both in Santa Cruz, those in La Laguna and La Orotava — as well as many private gardens. Deserving special mention are those belonging to some of the hotels in El Puerto de la Cruz, which grow exceedingly unusual species.

We will also see different varieties of the most beautiful flowers in all these places which have been duly classified by botanists. To mention a few: *Hibiscus rosa-sinensis,* a prolific bush of Chinese origin, popularly known as Hibiscus, which is found in many different colours although one normally sees it in red; *Datura chlorantha,* also known as ''yellow Dathura'' or ''moonflower'', supposedly from South America; even today its place of origin remains obscure. It has a deep yellow colour and intense perfume; *Strelitzia reginae* or ''bird of paradise'', typical of

Californian poppies and prickly pears.

Echiums and nasturtiums.

Tenerife and highly cultivated for decorative purposes as it lasts a very long time. It comes from South America; and *Euphorbia pulcherrima,* one of the most common tropical bushes popularly known as ''Poinsettia'' or ''Christmas flower'' which, however, comes from Mexico.

Other species of interest are: *Quisqualis indica,* a creeper from Southeast Asia, which is truly spectacular when in bloom; *Lonicera hildebrandiana,* also a creeper, the flowers of which are white when they blossom and an intense yellow as they wither; it is commonly known as honeysuckle; *Grevillea banksii,* an Australian plant with deep crimson colour flowers which bloom all the year around, its strange shape a warning of its danger, as it is known to produce strong allergies in some people; *Clivia miniata,* a decorative plant known as ''Clivia'' or ''Kafir lily'' which comes from South Africa; *Jasminum polianthum,* or ''Jasmine'', a creeper from China and Japan which has strongly scented flowers; *Bougainvillea glabra* and *Bougainvillea*

In Tenerife flowers of all kinds are grown, from the humble geraniums and lilies to the exotic orchids.

The red variety of hibiscus (hibiscus rosa sinensis) is the most common.

spectabilis, or ''Bougainvillaea'' from Brazil, with their exuberant blossoms; *Magnolia grandiflora,* ''Magnolia'' from the Southeast of the United States, its flowers giving off a soft and penetrating perfume; *Delonix regia,* or ''Flamboyant'', ''Flame tree'' or ''Royal poinciana'', with its very spectacular flowers; and finally the orchids, the most sought after for decorative purposes and which belong to the most numerous family in the plant kingdom. Although they are found all over the world, the vast majority are in the tropical and subtropical regions.

We can also include the famous plantation *the ''Bananera el Guanche''* in this section. It is in the city of La Orotava, only five minutes from El Puerto de la Cruz. A visit to this place is highly recommended as its 12,000 m^2 is covered with the most diverse species of plants and fruit trees. Thus, in perfectly ordered sections we find cocoa plants, tobacco, coffee, tomatoes, sugarcane, guava trees, avocado pears, papaya trees, custard apple and grapefruit trees, etc. The different types of cacti grown here are also of great interest. However, the

Wild specimens and brilliantly coloured
flowers, like this datura chlorantha or
moonflower.

Tenerife is one of the «fortunate islands» as its marvellous flora amply testify.

greatest tourist attraction is undoubtedly the banana plantation. The ''Bananera el Guanche'' offers us the opportunity of observing all the different stages in the growth of this fruit, which is so important for the economy of the island.

In the 15th century, a tall plant ressembling a palm tree, in fact, an inedible banana species from the Himalayan valleys, was brought for the first time to the archipelago as a botanical curiosity. It was only in 1855 that the Chinese banana or cavendish, also known as the dwarf banana, was introduced to the island by the French Consul in Santa Cruz de Tenerife, Sabin Berthelot.

The cultivation of bananas requires special care; the ground must first be prepared with a layer of volcanic gravel which assists drainage and ensures permeability. The plant takes a long time to grow, between 16 and 19 months depending on the amount of sunlight and water it receives as well as on the altitude of the plantation. The stem which bears the fruit grows downwards and can weigh from 15 to 60 kgs.

The strelitzia or bird of paradise flower
(strelitzia reginae).

Euphorbia pulchenima (Easter flower).

General view of Masca.

Landscape of Masca and the typical donkey ride. ▷

MASCA

Going back to our route, we can visit Garachico and the surrounding areas, and then travel into craggy, mountainous country, whose most representative spot is the secluded village, *Masca*. To reach it, we must turn off the main road at *El Moyedo* and go towards the coast on a local road. The difficulties faced initially are more than compensated for by the beautiful landscapes to be seen. The neighbouring areas can be explored on donkey-back, which makes the visit a truly unique experience.

Our stay in Masca amidst high mountains and deep ravines which make the place almost inaccessible will enable us to easily understand the need for the whistling language created by the Guanches, very widespread in the archipelago in the past. This language, which is still used in Gomera, allows long-distance communication through a series of whistles which have different meanings.

The Giants' Cliff, Puerto de Santiago.

PUERTO DE SANTIAGO: LOS GIGANTES CLIFF

Going back to the main road, we will soon arrive at a small village called *Tamaimo,* only a few kilometres away, where we can visit the small graveyard situated between lava deposits. At this point there is a turn off which leads to *Puerto de Santiago,* an important estate development which has an excellent leisure harbour.

The 63 m long Puerto de Santiago beach is 97 km away from the capital; its dark sand contrasts with the blue waters and the white surf.

The famous *Acantilado de los Gigantes* (cliff of the Giants) presides over this whole setting, offering a panoramic view of extraordinary beauty. This mass of basalt towers powerfully over the immense Atlantic ocean, braving the sea and giving the landscape a wholly unusual perspective.

The tourist may choose among all manner of hotels, apartments and shopping centres in addition to enjoying a wide beach of dark sands where he can not only rest but also practice different water sports, such as surfing, underwater fishing, etc.

If you stop for a long time in Puerto de

The beach at the foot of the cliffs and a detail of Puerto de Santiago.

From Puerto de Santiago we can enjoy a magnificent view of the Island of Gomera.

Panoramic view of the cliffs, which can be reached on a boat trip from the Playa de las Américas.

General view of the Giants' Coast with the Playa Arenas Negras in the foreground.

Santiago, there are numerous excursions you can make to nearby places. The road which brought us here leads to *Santiago del Teide,* a village set between poplars and cypresses, vineyards and fields where cereals are grown. A peculiar feature is its small parish church which has several cupolas vaguely reminiscent of a Moorish mosque.

Returning to Tamaimo, we can now travel into the interior on one of the roads leading to Las Cañadas del Teide National Park. This road goes through Mount Abeque and the Botija volcano, ending at the Boca Tauce pass. Finally, going south we arrive at *Guía de Isora,* at a height of 670 m. In this village of white houses surrounded by almond and walnut groves and small reservoirs, we can see a mastic tree, a deciduous tree from the tropical regions of America, and twin pines of large diameter in the Tágara pinewood. Before leaving this village, a visit to the parish church is recommended, where there is a carved image of the Christ of the ''Dulce Muerte''.

General view of the Playa de las Américas.

THE PLAYA DE LAS AMERICAS AND THE SURROUNDING AREAS

The *Playa de las Américas,* located in the districts of Arona and Adeje, ranks among the best international tourist resorts. Its waters are clean and transparent and its silver-grey sands, a reminder of the island's volcanic origin. The beach is lined with a row of palm trees reaching almost to the water's edge. Behind are the impressive hotel developments with swimming-pools and all manner of amenities designed to make your stay an enjoyable one.

The more adventurous could explore the area on the back of a camel.

Despite the arid and uninhabited panoramas characteristic of the southern part of the island, the gardens surrounding the developed areas create an overall colourful effect. From Playa de las Américas the nearby village of *Adeje* is easily reached. It once enjoyed great importance because its vast sugarcane plantations led to the owners constructing stately mansions there. A number of monuments of artistic interest dating from this period can be seen today, some of the most

*The Playa de las Américas provides us
with all we need in the way of relaxation
and amusement.*

Enjoy the sun and the sea on the Playa de las Américas.

outstanding being: the Franciscan monastery, the parish church of St. Ursula, where various Baroque reredoses and a beautiful polychrome coffered wooden ceiling can be admired, as well as the famous ''Casa-Fuerte'' the only surviving, rich stately mansion. It was built by the Ponte family who owned an immense sugarcane plantation cultivated by black slaves in the 16th century. It houses a large number of documents which give us a good idea of the customs and traditions of life on the island at the time.

However, it should not be forgotten that Adeje was first and foremost the place where the noble and legendary *mencey* Tinerfe lived, whose name translates as ''snow mountain''. The presence of the Guanches can still be felt in the unique *Barranco del Infierno* (Hell ravine) situated a few kilometres to the north. We highly recommend a visit to this unusual place which is one of the deepest chasms on the island, measuring 300 m, parts of which are so deep that the sun's rays have never penetrated them. The vegetation here

A camel ride is another of the attractions
of Playa de las Américas.

For several kilometres along the coast runs
a beautiful, lively pedestrian promenade
which joins the Playa de las Américas and
the Playa de los Cristianos.

In the early morning hours, Los Cristianos provides us with a wonderful show of light and colour.

LOS CRISTIANOS: THE TOURIST RESORT AND SURROUNDING AREAS

Los Cristianos, an old fishing village, is nowadays one of the most important tourist resorts in the south of the island as well as a magnificent choice for winter holidays thanks to its privileged geographical situation, its warm, unchanging climate all the year round and its long golden beaches and limpid waters.

Very little remains of the old and picturesque village as the skyline of Los Cristianos is today marked by hotels and modern estate developments, sweeping avenues and above all, by its outstanding port with moorings for as many as 200 boats. Besides the small fishing fleet, a large number of yachts and sailing boats are also moored here. The old fishermen's quarter nestles by mount Guaza, once a quarry from which paving stones exported to Cuba were obtained.

During our stay in Los Cristianos we can make excursions into the surrounding areas and so enjoy to the full the many other noteworthy places they have to offer.

General view of Los Cristianos.

Detail of the beautiful beach of Los Cristianos.

"Águilas del Teide" ecology park.

Near Mount Guaza you can find the charming Camel Park, and following the C-822 toward Añoma, visit the Águilas de Teide ecology park, a real paradise for plants and animals with more then 40 species of protected birds and many other animals. You can enjoy watching birds of prey in free flight, a spectacle that is unique in the world. A beautiful lake between rushes and palm-trees is home to swans, flamingos and other exquisite birds. Penguins delight visitors with their pirouettes and the elephant with her unexpected caresses. For the more intrepid, the park offers an entertaining means of transport in the form of the fast toboggan, as well as water scooters. You can see the exciting spectacle of the crocodiles being fed. In the park, you can enjoy the sun, and the magnificent sunsets, in any of the open-air cafés and restaurants, or take a romantic night-time walk to see owls and other species, or enjoy dinner in the splendid restaurant, in the form of an open-air amphitheatre surrounded by illuminated bridges over a lake of water-lilies. The park is open from 9 a.m. to 7 p.m., and again from 7.30 p.m. for the evening session. A free bus runs from Los Cristianos and Las Américas every day, from Los Gigantes on Sundays, and from Tembel on Mondays and Fridays.

On the coast of silence, a detail of the Tenbel tourist centre.

areas. We can enjoy an underwater trip in the only submarine in the world equipped for this purpose. This exotic vehicle has the appealing name of "Yellow Submarine". Lastly, it is worth visiting *Punta Rasca,* from where you have impressive panoramic views of the coast and the sea.

Heading towards Santa Cruz de Tenerife on the motorway, we go past the prestigious *Aeropuerto Transoceánico Reina Sofía,* which is equipped with comfortable installations and now handles all international flights. It also boasts more air traffic and greater capacity than most European airports. We will then arrive at the beautiful, white beaches of Confital, La Tejita and *El Médano.* The latter, which has more than 3 km of golden sands and has been completely developed, is one of the most popular beaches on the island.

For those who wish to go on boat trips, the nearby island of *La Gomera* can be visited from Los Cristianos. There is a regular ferry and speed-boat service, with large and comfortable seating accommodation that make the crossing in a relatively short time.

El Médano beach.

The Church of Our Lady of Candlemas.

THE GÜIMAR VALLEY AND CANDELARIA

Going back to Santa Cruz de Tenerife, we can make our way to two important small towns. The south road, or even the motorway, will take us first to *Güimar,* with its inviting squares and streets and its small, beautiful parish church. Nearby is the so-called ''Puertito de Güimar'' which has been transformed into an important tourist spot, well equipped with hotels and sports facilities. However, Güimar is famous above all because of its valley, geographically similar to La Orotava valley, and its volcano or Montaña Grande which has a circumference of 300 m and a depth of 60 m.

Further on, we will arrive at the small town of *Candelaria,* whose history, wrapped in legend, has made it one of the most important places of pilgrimage and devotion on the island.

According to the chronicles, in the latter part of the 14th century, a statue of the Virgin Mary was washed up by the waves onto the shores of the Chimisay beaches, exactly where the town stands. The *mencey* of Güimar recovered it and kept it in his cave where it stayed for almost half a cen-